BRITAIN IN OLD PHOTOGRAPHS

FIFE
AT WORK

CAROL McNEILL

D0177049

The
History
Press

CONTENTS

ACKNOWLEDGEMENTS

Very many thanks to all the people and organisations who helped with information or images for this book, or who listened patiently to my many questions about local industries. These include Burntisland Heritage Trust, Dysart Trust, Fife Mining Heritage Society, Jim Fraser, Kinghorn Historical Society, Kirkcaldy Civic Society, Bob Kilgour, Ian Lindsay, the Local and Family History Department at Kirkcaldy Galleries, Michael Martin, Photopolis.org, RCAHMS, Chris Sparling, Don Swanson, and Eddie Wellcoat.

ABOUT THE AUTHOR

Former journalist Carol McNeill has a lifelong interest in local history and has written twenty illustrated books about Kintyre, where she was born and brought up, and Fife, where she now lives.

INTRODUCTION

Fife, on the east coast of Scotland, has a proud heritage of traditional industries, most of which have sadly disappeared over the passage of time. These ranged from heavy industry such as mining, shipbuilding, textile mills, floorcloth, blacksmiths, engineering, and pottery to the manufacture of almost everything from huge engines to golf clubs, as well as industries relating to rural life such as farming and fishing: just some of the avenues of employment open to Fife folk.

A few of these industries still remain, although their working conditions and methods have changed; but the majority have gone forever. Kinghorn and Burntisland shipbuilders no longer make huge cargo vessels for Australia or Chile; there is no call now for Dysart manufacturers to make linen for pioneer America's covered wagons; the whalers have – thankfully – stopped landing their catches from the Arctic at Kirkcaldy harbour; and deep coal mining which was one of Fife's main industries ended in 1988 with the closure of Seafield pit.

Although it is not within the scope of this book to record every type of industry in depth, it is important to give at least a snapshot of some of these traditional industries and ways of life which gave so many people employment, and which helped Fife to make an important contribution not only to this country but in many cases throughout the world.

The fishing industry at one time played an important part in Fife's economy; many of the towns and villages in east Fife such as St Andrews, Crail, St Monans, Anstruther, Buckhaven, Largo and Pittenweem had their own fishing fleets. Buckhaven was reported in 1831 to have the largest fishing fleet in Scotland with 198 boats; in 1881 there were 400 fishermen living in Buckhaven, many of whom were 'free fishers' who owned their own homes, boats and fishing gear. Sometimes the boats went to Whitby or South Shields using big lines for herring bait, and then it was the 'summer drave' when they went to Peterhead from June to August. Buckhaven boatbuilder David Brown made the *Fifie* which was followed by the *Baldie* and then the *Zulu*, but the sailing boats eventually gave way to the steam drifters in the early 1900s. Local fishermen all wore 'ganseys' or guernseys, heavy knitted jerseys which were worn with oilskins or canvas jerkins in bad weather.

Scottish Fisheries Museum in Anstruther has a wonderful collection of historic fishing boats and fishing gear, which illustrate the daily lives of those who lived in the fishing communities. It tells the story of how Scottish fishermen played such a vital part of Scotland's tradition and heritage.

Coal has been mined in Fife virtually since records began, with rich seams of coal underground or even near the surface throughout much of the county. There were coalfields in central, west and east Fife including Buckhaven, Comrie, Cowdenbeath, Crossgates, Cupar, Dunfermline, Dunnikier, Dysart, Glenrothes, Lochgelly, Lochore, Methil, Kinglassie, Kirkcaldy, Wemyss, Muiredge, Methilhill, and Thornton. The list seems endless and even these were not the only coalfields which gave employment to many thousands of men (and in the early days women and even children). Mining is a dangerous and difficult occupation and the mining communities were of necessity very close-knit areas: what affected one family, affected all. Before nationalisation in 1946, which brought all the collieries under the National Coal Board, the mines were owned by land owners whose estates held rich mineral seams.

Fertile land throughout Fife has always been ideal for farming, a way of life which involved the whole family, with farms often being passed down through the generations. One Fife woman recalled:

My father worked on an estate as a forester and then as the money was very poor my father took on farm work and drove the horses. It meant we had a rent-free house and garden and got so many potatoes per year. The farmers took on everybody, Irishmen came over every year to thin turnips and then the harvest. They lived in a bothy which had two 'ends', a place for eating and a place for sleeping on straw mattresses. The local farm workers' houses were fairly good, sometimes just a room and kitchen and other times two rooms upstairs, but only outside sanitation. Some workers had cows but they would have to pay for the feeding.

The farming communities worked alongside dairies, blacksmiths, saddlers and harness makers, which all provided specialised and vital services.

With much of the east coast of Fife bordering the river Forth, it's not surprising that shipping and shipbuilding played a vital role in the local economy. Kirkcaldy harbour was established as early as the sixteenth century; James V is recorded as leaving there in 1536 with seven ships, and the Marquis of Montrose sailed from Kirkcaldy to Leith to be tried on Monday in Edinburgh and executed on Tuesday.

Kirkcaldy also had a local fleet of whaling vessels, including *Hecla*, *Triad*, *Chieftain*, *Caledonia*, *Viewforth*, *Abram* and *Lord Gambier*. It was a dangerous way to earn a living: *Abram*, *Lord Gambier* and *Chieftain* were all trapped in ice although their crews were eventually rescued. Contemporary reports of their cargoes make difficult reading today: in one season in 1833, for example, the whalers brought home 900 tons of whale oil and 60 tons of whalebone.

At one time Kirkcaldy was a very busy commercial port giving employment to large numbers of workers. Harbour records for 1938 give an indication of the huge loads which were being offloaded then including 32,000 tons of cement, 7,100 tons of wood, with 9,400 tons of linseed oil and 18,077 tons of cork for the linoleum industry. Ships such as MV *Atlantic Coast* and MV *Welsh Coast* brought cement from London to serve the building trade, and in the 1950s there were several large builders merchants' warehouses round the harbour. One single development contributed to the decline of the harbour: when a Dunbar plant started to manufacture cement, this no longer had to be imported and a huge part of the harbour trade disappeared.

Methil was the chief coal port in Scotland just after the First World War; its first dock was designed by engineers Gibson and Hopewell and opened in May 1887. The second and third docks were opened in 1913, financed by Randolph Wemyss and later taken over by the North British Railway Company. A branch line from the main Thornton to Buckhaven railway line ran straight down to the docks to facilitate transport. Dysart harbour too was a hugely important port in the eighteenth and nineteenth centuries; older people with long memories could remember the days when the harbour was packed solid with tall-masted sailing ships from Holland, France and the Netherlands; even in the 1920s it was commonplace to see a dozen ships in the harbour with several others lying off the pier waiting for their turn for a docking space.

Shipbuilding flourished for many years in Kinghorn, Burntisland, Kirkcaldy and Dysart. The Abden Shipbuilding Yard in Kinghorn was founded in 1863 by John Key, a Kirkcaldy-based engineer who manufactured his marine engines at Whitebank foundry and transported them by special train to Kinghorn. The yard itself was situated next door to the parish church with a slipway down to the Forth – presumably Sunday was a day of rest, otherwise the minister would have struggled to be heard over the ringing of heavy industry. One of the best known of the Abden Yard's ships was the paddle-driven passenger ferry *William Muir*, which made regular crossings from Burntisland to Granton for many years; she was thought to have made around 80,000 crossings of the Forth until she was scrapped in 1937. It comes as a surprise now to realise that the small and picturesque seaside town of Kinghorn built twenty ships for Australia as well as vessels for London, Glasgow, Malta, Singapore and Spain. When John Key died in 1876, the yard passed to his sons before being taken over and modernised by John Scott, finally closing down in 1922.

The Burntisland Shipbuilding Company Ltd was founded by the Ayre brothers from Tyneside in 1918 and built 310 ships – including cargo ships, steamers and self-trimming coal ships – during its lifetime of just over fifty years. The yard weathered the downturn in trade in the 1960s fairly well, but was dealt a hammer blow in 1968 when the construction of the cargo liner *Ohrmazd* came up against wrangles over contracts and specifications between the yard and the ship owners. This meant delays in construction which in turn led to financial penalties. The ship was eventually completed but the yard went into liquidation in 1968, building another two ships before it closed down completely. In Kirkcaldy there were at least two shipyards, one owned by the Swan Brothers at the Bucket Pats at the east end of the harbour, and Brown's shipyard at the Tiel Burn, operating in the 1860s. Dysart's yard at the harbour built everything from small cargo vessels to large schooners and was said to be the largest shipyard in Fife by the late nineteenth century. On a smaller but equally important scale, James Miller & Sons' yard in St Monans built wooden fishing boats and yachts for more than 200 years before closing in 1995.

Textile production was one of Fife's earliest industries, starting off with handloom weaving being carried out in cottages in towns and villages. Dunfermline was noted for its fine quality of bed and table linen including fine silk production, Kirkcaldy and Dysart had several large textile mills, and Falkland was one of the earliest textile producers. Linen workers were said to be of strong political persuasions; fibres from the flax used were processed by workers known as hecklers who became well versed in interrupting meetings with their political views. The term heckler, still used for those who make their views on a subject loudly known, is thought to have originated from the early linen workers.

Before the days of plastic dishes and aluminium teapots, potteries were a vital part of the domestic economy. Kirkcaldy had four main potteries, three in the Gallatown area and one in Linktown (originally a separate burgh). The distinctive kilns with their smoking chimneys were a feature of the trade which produced so much pottery, both for industrial and domestic use.

The largest pottery was David Methven & Sons' Kirkcaldy Pottery, situated on a large sprawling site in the Links area of the town. Morrison and Crawford, Sinclairtown Pottery, and Robert Heron & Son's Fife Pottery were all within a stone's throw of each other and well away from the centre of town. Although the finished ceramic products were colourful and delicate, the firing of the kilns during manufacture – with up to 12 tons of coal to fire a single kiln – produced a great deal of heavy smoke and pollution.

Each firm had their own specialities but Fife Pottery produced Wemyss Ware with beautifully decorated pieces which are now highly prized and can fetch eye-watering prices at auction. Although Wemyss Ware started out producing self-coloured vases and cups based on items belonging to the Wemyss family in nearby Wemyss Castle, this was only the start. A local paper in 1882 commented, 'A few of the flower vases are embellished with local views by the firm's own artist. The new ware is likely to be as great a favourite as the black hand-painted enamelled ware for which the Messrs. Heron are so famous'. The writer of that newspaper article could have had no idea at the time of just how 'great a favourite' this experimental Wemyss Ware was to become.

The inspiration for the ware came from artist Karel Nekola from Bohemia who was head-hunted by Robert Heron, who recognised his outstanding artistic talent. A highly skilled and imaginative artist, Nekola painted apples, cherries, forget-me-nots, birds and his classic cabbage roses, transforming quite utilitarian items such as toilet sets, fingerplates, doorknobs and vases into beautiful pieces of art. His sons Joseph and Carl also worked in Fife Pottery and other major artists included Edwin Sandland, James Sharp and David Grinton.

Fife is renowned for its fine golf courses, with the Old Course in St Andrews having a world-famous reputation; countless numbers of golf enthusiasts flock there every year as well as to the other excellent courses. The legendary 'Old' Tom Morris, who was born in 1821, won four Open Championships between 1861 and 1867 and played in every British Open until 1895. He also made his own golf clubs and balls and helped to design golf courses in many parts of the country. Although the Old Course can be seen at the top of every golfer's wish list to play on, there are many other excellent courses in Fife which are enjoyed by both amateur golfers and professionals.

For many years the name of Kirkcaldy was synonymous with linoleum, with the distinctive smell of linseed oil giving rise to *The Boy in the Train*, a poem by Mary Campbell Smith which had the famous last words 'For I ken mysel' by the queer-like smell, that the next stop's Kirkcaddy!' The pioneer in the town's linoleum industry was Michael Nairn, who built his first canvas factory in Coal Wynd in the back garden of his house in the High Street. He graduated from there to building a large factory on the Path stretching down to Pathhead sands, where he set about making floorcloth. This venture was looked on with a mixture of scorn and amazement by local people who immediately termed it 'Nairn's Folly'. They saw it as a foolish venture but how wrong they were: Nairn made sure the factory was near the main railway line and also the harbour, where he could import cork and linseed oil and export his linoleum all over the world – and indeed, the rest is history. Barry, Ostlere and Shepherd Ltd – an amalgamation of the earlier businesses of Kirkcaldy Linoleum Company Ltd and John Barry, Ostlere and Company Ltd – were also important linoleum manufacturers in the town with several factories. And for many years a linoleum factory owned by the Scottish Co-operative Wholesale Society operated in the rural village of Falkland. Floor covering of a different nature came to Dysart when James Meikle set up a carpet factory in a disused linen mill, adjusting the old looms and training the staff in each process required to make quality material. The firm made wool-reversible carpets which as well as being comfortable and hard-wearing, had the added bonus of being able to be turned over when the carpet started to wear. Three of James Meikle's daughters – Janet,

Isobel and Margaret – joined the firm and later became directors, and Meikle's carpets are still wearing well in many homes both in this country and abroad.

The changing shape of retail has altered drastically over recent years. Large stores and internet shopping have largely replaced the small independent shops which used to make up most of Fife's retail landscape. A look back at how High Streets used to look can be quite a trip down memory lane.

Although some of these traditional industries have survived, often in a different form, many sadly are now no longer in operation – but there are traces of them still visible for those who take the time to look. Fortunately, the coastal villages, rural settings and individual towns have always made Fife a popular tourist destination; its sandy beaches, golf courses, historic buildings and beautiful countryside attract many visitors, many of whom return year after year.

Carol McNeill
Fife, 2016

1

FISHING

This photograph of Anstruther from the west in the early 1900s shows the large fleet of fishing boats tied up at the pier. There used to be occasional rivalry among the fishing villages along the east coast; a Dysart man recalled meeting a fisherman in Anstruther who said, 'Your haddocks are getting to the right size, we'll be down to clear them out' – and they did.

The Harbour, Anstruther.

The Morning Catch at Largo

14

Landing the Catch, Cargo

There was plenty of help on hand and an audience of local people when the small sailing boats came into the pier with the day's haul of fish. Live shellfish were kept in boxes submerged in the harbour until they were needed to bait the fishing lines. Fishermen's nets can be seen hung out to dry on poles on the other bank.

Opposite above: Anstruther near St Andrews is one of a string of fishing villages along the Fife coast in what is known as the East Neuk, with a horse and cart with a cargo of coal providing the only transport of the day before cars took over. The masts of the fishing boats can be seen tied up at the pier with the letters KY denoting Kirkcaldy.

Opposite below: Lower Largo was another bustling fishing village in the East Neuk and there was always a crowd of fishermen and villagers to view the morning catch and assess its value. Some of the fish was sold locally, with the fresh catch being taken round the doors on hand-barrows.

Overleaf: This image shows women in the fishermen's quarter at St Andrews harbour shelling mussels for bait. One woman recalled, 'Shelling mussels was a heartbreaking job in winter, the knife went into the mussel, wheeled round and scooted out again, by that time you were soaking.'

Local fishing boats are seen here tied up at St Andrews harbour after the day's catch, with the ancient St Rule's Tower on the Cathedral grounds in the background. The fishermen went to Peterhead from June to August for the 'summer drave' and then they went to Yarmouth in October until the beginning of December.

The distinctive sail-driven boats in the Fife fishing fleets included the *Fifie* with its vertical stem and square sail, *Zulu* and *Baldie* (named after the Italian Garibaldi). Ring net fishing was much more successful than the earlier drift nets and brought in much larger catches.

Joan Clark, thought to be the last fishwife in St Andrews, wheeled her barrow round the streets until the 1920s selling freshly caught fish. She wore the traditional striped skirt and white apron, red knitted bodice with a shawl, and spotless white stockings with elastic-sided boots. 'I remember going to Edinburgh and seeing two Newhaven fishwives standing at the corner of the Mound selling whelks and mussels, fourpence for a saucer – food for the gods,' recalled one local man.

Elie fishermen's traditional cottage on the shore with one of the young generation lending a hand. The fishing lines, with hundreds of small hooks baited with shelled mussels, had to be constantly checked to keep them free from tangles. A local man recalled, 'The women kept baiting the lines through the day with the mussels, what a speed they went at.'

The Toft area near the harbour in Elie was the traditional fishermen's quarter. They were able to use the sandy area to spread out their nets and the rest of their gear to dry before their next trip to sea. It was a hard and often dangerous way of life where much of the success rested on the weather, the tides and the skills of knowing the best places to drop their nets.

St Monans was another busy East Neuk fishing port with more than 400 fishermen working there in the late 1920s. James M. Miller & Sons' boatyard, founded in the eighteenth century, built beautifully crafted wooden yachts and boats suitable for modern fishing for 200 years before the business closed down.

Lower Largo was another busy fishing village, with this view taken from the railway viaduct showing the picturesque harbour and the Crusoe Hotel. Fishing nets hanging out to dry can be seen on the right. Largo is still a favourite spot for tourists, especially during the summer months.

The Harbour, St. Andrews

This view of St Andrews harbour shows a fleet of fishing boats tied up at the pier with the old Royal George tenement and Bell Rock Tavern on the quayside and the gasworks chimney towering behind. The harbour front has now been carefully restored.

21

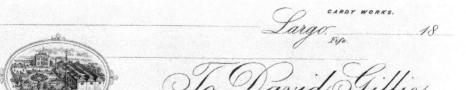

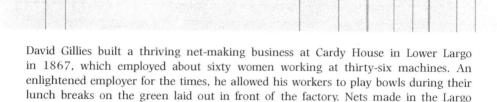

To David Gillies.

(Net Manufacturer.)

TERMS FOR NETS: PER CENT OFF FOR READY CASH ON DELIVERY OF THE NETS, OR   PER CENT OFF AT END OF FIRST FISHING.

NO DISCOUNT ALLOWED IF NOT PAID AT END OF FIRST FISHING, AND AFTER THAT ONE SHILLING PER NET ADDED PER ANNUM.

David Gillies built a thriving net-making business at Cardy House in Lower Largo in 1867, which employed about sixty women working at thirty-six machines. An enlightened employer for the times, he allowed his workers to play bowls during their lunch breaks on the green laid out in front of the factory. Nets made in the Largo factory were sent as far as Melbourne, Australia.

This image shows the traditional area for Buckhaven fishermen in West Shore Street near the harbour. Their houses, which had the distinctive forestairs, were clustered together close to their boats, and the fishermen hung out their nets and bladders to dry on posts on the shore while their wives gave the household washing an airing.

Opposite above: These small cottages, pictured in the early 1900s near Buckhaven's Harbour Head, were known as the West End and would have been originally occupied by fishermen and their families. Although picturesque with their traditional pantiled roofs, the cottages would have been basic in the extreme with little in the way of modern conveniences.

Opposite below: The *Reaper* is a 70ft Fifie sailing herring drifter, first registered in Fraserburgh in 1902 and bought in the 1970s by the Scottish Fisheries Museum. Originally built as a sailing lugger, she had an engine installed for the first time in 1916. Beautifully restored to her original condition, she is today crewed by volunteers and visits ports round Scotland and Northern England and is pictured here in Dysart harbour.

Locals gathered to pass the time of day and catch up with news on West Shore Street in Anstruther, which had a ships' chandler's business on the corner. The Williamson Memorial drinking fountain was dedicated to Stephen Williamson, founder of the Balfour Williamson Shipping Line and MP for St Andrews Burghs.

Crail harbour, a picturesque spot then as now, is pictured here in the 1930s with local men busy loading boxes of fish on to a hand-cart ready to take their catch to local markets. The old houses with their vernacular architecture have since been sensitively restored. There is still commercial fishing from the harbour for crab and lobster, which have a fine reputation for quality.

Another view of the historic old houses clustered round Crail harbour, with fishing boats in the water and some drawn up to dry in the sun. An ancient Royal Burgh, Crail has been a prosperous fishing port since the twelfth century and its tranquility and old-world charm make it a favourite spot for tourists and photographers.

At one time Dysart men fished for salmon in the Forth, but these fish have now long gone. This rare old image shows the salmon nets drying opposite the old houses at Pan Ha, which were carefully restored by the National Trust for Scotland in 1969 without losing any of their character. The restoration was marked by a visit from the Queen Mother, who unveiled a commemorative plaque in her capacity as Patron of the National Trust for Scotland.

The fleet of fishing boats at Anstruther harbour before they set off in search of the silver darlings, as the herring were nicknamed. With the fishing villages tending to be close-knit, it was common for fishermen's daughters to marry within the local community.

This panoramic view of Anstruther taken from the Chalmers Lighthouse includes the lifeboat slip and boatyard. A travelling fair with a roundabout and children's entertainments can also be seen on the pier.

2

MINING

The Denbeath Colliery was sunk in the 1870s and leased by Bowman and Company until their tenancy ran out in 1905, when it was taken over by the Wemyss Coal Company and renamed the Wellesley. The coal washer, said to be one of the largest in the country, was built as part of the company's investment. The pit complex was enlarged in 1907 with a new shaft and increased production before it closed in 1967.

Methil was very much a coal community, with mining and its ancillaries providing employment to a huge number of local people. Methil's Main Street was dominated by the Wellesley colliery buildings, a constant reminder of the importance of mining in the area.

There were three pits in full production in Dysart in the 1850s: the Randolph, the Lady Blanche and the Frances Colliery (pictured), known locally as the Dubbie. In 1958 the Frances employed 1,400 men and produced 2,000 tons of coal a day. A section of the pit which stretched three-quarters of a mile under the Forth had one of the highest production rates in the UK.

In 1980 the coalfields at the Dubbie – which by then had the distinction of being Scotland's oldest working pit – and nearby Seafield were linked under the Forth. This image shows the start of the damage done to the once sandy beach when more and more colliery waste, or redd, from the Frances was dumped on the foreshore. The small building in the centre was a popular café during the summer months.

Miners are pictured underground at the Frances Colliery in 1942, a rare image as it was unusual for the men to be photographed at work near the coal face. Although rumours of the pit's closure were active in 1982, miners were assured that their jobs were safe, but in 1985 the National Coal Board announced that the Frances was to close with the loss of 500 jobs.

Minto Colliery, locally known as Brigghills, was one of several pits in the Lochgelly area. Earmarked for closure in 1963, it was saved briefly thanks to the efforts of the miners to increase profitability, but eventually underground fires closed the colliery down.

Lochgelly was very much a mining town with the local economy heavily dependent on the wages from the collieries. The men pictured here were probably miners congregating for a chat in Main Street between working on their shifts below ground.

Muiredge Pit in Buckhaven was owned by Bowman and Company with three shafts operational by 1879. It stopped production in 1932 when it was used to train young miners until it closed three years later. The Randolph Wemyss Memorial Hospital in Denbeath opened in 1909 and was donated by Lady Eva Wemyss, widow of Randolph Wemyss, originally to treat injured miners.

Lochgelly station, with one of the town's pits just visible in the background on the left of the photograph. After the collieries closed down, an extensive programme of regeneration and clearing took place in and around the town under a coalfields regeneration scheme.

An underground fire tragedy at Hill of Beath Colliery in Cowdenbeath in 1901 caused the death of seven miners; tragically this was just one of many mining accidents throughout the country before health and safety rules were enforced.

A Dunnikier coal wagon from the Pannie pit in the Smeaton area of Kirkcaldy. This pit was sunk around the 1880s and closed in April 1927, although the pit bing was left there for some time. There was a bleach field on the site after the pit closed, and it's thought that the Home Guard may have used the ground for training during the Second World War.

A line of coal wagons are pictured at Inverkeithing harbour, with a fleet of Fifies in the bay, possibly laid up there at the end of the fishing season. The railway network was essential in transferring coal from the pit heads to factories, businesses and homes.

High Binn village above Burntisland consisted of ninety-five two-roomed houses which were built for workers in the Binnend shale mine and oil works. When they closed down in 1893 most of the workers left and troops were billeted there in the First World War, with the houses still occupied – many as holiday homes – in the early twentieth century.

The smaller Low Binn was built nearer the main road and seems to have been considered at the time to be the inferior settlement of the two, perhaps because of its more transient population. The waterlogged ground in front of the houses must have caused health problems.

Preparatory work sinking a shaft under the Forth began in 1954 and production started at Seafield Colliery in Kirkcaldy in 1965. Five miners were tragically killed in a roof collapse in a mining tragedy in May 1973. There was an earlier pit, Seafield Mine, on much the same site from 1923 to 1930, with a plaque commemorating this erected by Kirkcaldy Civic Society and Fife Mining Heritage Society.

Although at its peak Seafield employed more than 2,450 miners, the colliery closed down for good in 1988. Demolition of the pit complex, including the twin landmark towers, took place over a period of two weekends in September 1989.

Preparation for the demolition was rigorous as it was essential to get the technical process absolutely right while making sure that safety was paramount both for the demolition team and for the surrounding area. Part of the main road from Kirkcaldy to Kinghorn had to be closed while the blasting process took place.

The actual demolition only lasted a couple of minutes on two consecutive weekends, with crowds of local people congregating to watch at strategic viewing points. Clearing the site was a lengthy process, and an estate of houses with views of the Forth now stands on the site.

This group photo was taken at Buckhaven in 1918 at one of the annual Miners' Galas, with a member of the Logie family in the centre of the front row. The Galas were important occasions to the mining communities: one former miner recalled, 'The Miners' Gala Day was the first Monday in June, a red letter day. We usually packed into a train for Edinburgh or Perth or wherever the rally was being held, then back home for a street party in the town square.'

The Frances Memorial in Edington Place, Dysart, was dedicated to the men and women who worked in the Dysart pit from 1873 onwards. There are mining memorials throughout Fife including Buckhaven and Kirkcaldy for those who tragically died at the underground fire disaster at the Michael Colliery in September 1967 and over a period of years at Seafield.

3

FARMING

Two horses and carts with the village of Strathkinness spread out behind them showing its rich farming land. Many of the buildings seen in this photograph would be farmsteads or homes to people who worked on the land. Farmers depended on heavy horsepower before mechanisation helped to lighten the workload.

Heavy horses were used for rolling and harrowing on this Dunfermline farm. One woman recalled her first job when she left school at 12: 'There were seven of us youngsters started at the same time hoeing beans, potatoes and turnips. When the haytime came we helped with that, then it was the harvest when we worked from 6 a.m. to 6 p.m. and left the fields at 12 to go home for our dinners.'

DYKE NEUK, LEVEN.

Dyke Neuk near Leven was typical of many smallholdings which kept hens and chickens to supply their own needs. An unusual sight beside this little cottage are the miniature houses placed in the hedges, probably as hives for bees or as coops for domestic pigeons.

There is now no trace of Hayfield Farm in Kirkcaldy, which was still in existence in the 1930s. It was originally called Hungerfield Farm and was renamed by Dr Hay, the last owner of the farm. The area is now built over with housing and shops in a busy part of the town with Hayfield Road the only reminder of this rural scene.

The Agricultural show in Cupar around 1900 drew large crowds of visitors, with keenly contested classes as well as trade stands with commercial exhibits of interest to the rural community. It was also an occasion for ladies to put on their best dresses and show off their parasols, with the men in suits and hats or flat caps. Some new-fangled bicycles can be seen among the horses.

Highland Agricultural Show, Cupar 1912

The annual Highland Show (before it added Royal to its name) was held in different locations, including Cupar in 1912. This image shows heavy horses being paraded before the judges with a largely male audience. There was a good selection of trade stands round the grounds including exhibits of farming machinery, foodstuffs, and fertilisers including Lawes Chemical Manure.

THE WESTERN DISTRICT OF FIFE AGRICULTURAL SOCIETY

(FORMED IN 1765)

Catalogue of Entries

FOR

ANNUAL SHOW

SOUTH FOD FARM, DUNFERMLINE,

(By courtesy of F. SIMPSON, Esq.)

SATURDAY, 1st JULY, 1961.

Price - 2/-

The Committee request that Members whose Subscriptions are still unpaid will pay them at the Secretary's Tent in the Showyard.

R. K. LINDSAY & Co., DUNFERMLINE

The programme from the Western District of Fife Agricultural Society in July 1961 listed a huge range of specialised entries including shorthorn bulls, Ayrshire heifers, best-groomed workhorse, pigs and sheepdogs as well as baking and floral art. The show was hotly contested by country folk and the competition for top prizes in each section was often fierce.

St Monans was mainly a fishing village but the fertile land here and in the East Neuk also supported farming communities. 'In my young days, the farm workers' houses were good but of course they had no indoor sanitation,' recalled a Fife woman. 'Floors were cement, the interior was pretty rough and we had to provide our own furniture.'

The blacksmith, or smiddy, played an important part in rural villages, including Strathkinness where horses were a necessity for both farming and transport. Blacksmith William Young, pictured here with his wife Margaret and young son, lived there from around 1891 to the 1920s.

The smiddy in Coaltown of Wemyss provided a vital service for the Wemyss villages and further afield. The blacksmith with his leather apron is pictured with one of his newly forged horseshoes, with members of his family beside him and some of his workers in the background.

Although Ballingry and Lochore were primarily mining areas, there were still farms and fields in the area. Farmworkers in Fife who could afford to keep a pig fed it up through the year and then killed it for pork and hams; hams hung from hooks in the ceiling to dry and provided meat for some time.

Chapel village was once a farming community and a separate hamlet from Kirkcaldy, although it is now a part of the burgh. The land originally belonged to the Oswalds of Dunnikier, and most of the houses would be for agricultural workers. Almost all of the buildings in the foreground, including the smiddy, have now disappeared.

MacLeod's saddlers and harness makers in Dysart supplied farms in different parts of Fife with vital equipment for the farmers' daily lives. The owner, James MacLeod (pictured at the right of the front door), became Provost of Dysart in 1919, a position he held until 1930 when Dysart amalgamated with Kirkcaldy.

Lawson's Dairy in East High Street in Buckhaven kept a fine herd of cows on the premises, ensuring that customers got fresh milk every morning. Although environmental health laws now would never allow such a situation, it was commonplace in the early 1900s for dairies to have their own cattle in the same place as the milk was produced.

This farm in Newton of Balcormo near Anstruther in north-east Fife made the most of the fine weather to dry the stooks of corn. One man recalled that there were hiring fairs on 28 May, called term day, where workers looked for new posts where they stayed at least until the same time next year.

Auchtermuchty farm is pictured with a good field of traditional haystacks and a well-worn farm track in the foreground. Taking in the harvest was always a busy time with much depending on good weather conditions. Many farmers preferred hiring married men so that their wives and children could help with the work

4

SHIPPING AND
SHIPBUILDING

The Docks, Burntisland.

Burntisland dock was second only to Leith in importance as a seaport on the River Forth and its position was strengthened with the opening of a wet dock in 1876. The shipment of coal reached a record of almost 2.5 million tons in 1913, but decreased during the First World War.

Dysart harbour was a busy port in the eighteenth and nineteenth centuries, with tall ships bringing in timber, linseed oil, wine and iron from Rotterdam and Hamburg and exporting ironstone, salt and coal to Aberdeen, Perth and Montrose. There was a set scale of charges for ships coming in and out, and in the late nineteenth century there would be eight tall ships in port each day with another two or three often foreign ships anchored in the Forth.

A tall ship anchored in Kirkcaldy dock around the 1900s. Sailors' Walk, the building opposite the harbour, was built in the sixteenth century. It was spared demolition in the 1930s when a far-seeing local group launched a public appeal to save it. Original features were uncovered including a wooden ceiling decorated with fish and flowers, beams inscribed with Biblical texts, fleur-de-lis and thistles in plasterwork, and a wooden bed which slid into a stone recess.

Methil was one of the chief coal ports in Scotland just after the First World War, exporting more than 3 million tons annually by 1923. The docks were linked directly to the Wellesley pit and a branch rail link had marshalling yards and coal loading facilities. This ship from Hamburg was typical of the overseas ships which used the dock, which had so many foreign visitors that both a Norwegian and German Mission were set up in the town for the sailors.

West Wemyss harbour, dating from the sixteenth century, is pictured with its visiting tall-masted ships. It exported thousands of tons of coal annually, mainly to Scandinavia and England until the local Lady Emma and the Victoria pits closed down.

A great storm in October 1898 drove the Norwegian ship *AW Singleton* off course from Gothenburg to Methil and dashed her on the rocks below Wemyss Castle. The wreck attracted the attention of local boys who clambered aboard the vessel without realising that the tide had come in; they were duly rescued but not before they got a thorough telling-off from their mothers.

Aberdour's silver sands drew crowds of visitors during the summer months with paddle steamers calling in regularly at the stone pier. In 1908 a nearby tearoom welcomed tourists and advertised 'Picnics and parties purveyed for; good accommodation for cyclists.'

PIPE BAND, "MARS."

Above and overleaf: The *Mars* was a former battleship for vulnerable boys needing supervision or protection who were then trained in various crafts such as joinery, gardening and tailoring under strict naval discipline. They had an annual holiday in coastal resorts such as Elie where they had the freedom to take part in sports on the beach and also gave concerts to local audiences.

ROPE SPLICI

MARS.

The *Mars* took in 6,500 boys over the course of sixty years. Their training must have been hard at times, but their years on the ship also put many of the youngsters on the right track for their adult lives. The ship was decommissioned in 1929 and this image shows the ship being taken to Inverkeithing for breaking up, watched by one of the officers and some of the boys.

Kirkcaldy harbour was an important port for several hundred years with a bustling import and export trade, particularly for the linoleum business. The ship at the centre back with the chevron on her funnel was one of the Coast Line vessels which regularly brought in cement for the building industry.

Kirkcaldy Harbour Head is pictured with ships including the *John Strachan* from Kirkcaldy on the left. The nearby Harbourhead Hotel provided a useful service for seamen in port between voyages. Some of the town's many factory chimneys can be seen in the background.

Kirkcaldy harbour was a bustling place in the 1950s. A branch railway with a swing bridge to let ships through was built in 1849 to increase commercial traffic, particularly for the linoleum industry. Nairn's St Mary's works can be seen in the background.

A goods train pulled by a steam engine regularly went over the bridge at the foot of the Path on a branch line to the harbour. On one occasion still remembered by some local people the train ran away and plunged into the harbour with the driver and fireman able to jump clear just in time.

This section of Kirkcaldy harbour was locally known as the 'wee pier' as smaller boats were able to tie up easily here as well as boats from the local sailing club. As the town's industries decreased, trade diminished and the entire harbour lay unused for many years in the late twentieth century. It has re-opened to commercial shipping recently to service the expanding flour mill at the foot of the Path.

The beautiful old two-masted brig *Phoenix*, built in Denmark in 1929, now features in many period dramas. She moored in Dysart in 2015 as part of the film set for the *Outlander* series of films and has appeared in many other films including *Frenchman's Creek*, *Moll Flanders*, *Poldark* and *Dr Who*.

Dysart had a flourishing shipbuilding trade at the harbour which was reported as early as 1764, and in the late nineteenth century was considered to be the largest shipyard in Fife. The yard produced a large number of ships over the course of 150 years or so, under several owners including John Watt, who took over the yard in the 1860s to build wooden ships such as fishing boats and tall-masted schooners. This image shows the yard with a schooner under construction.

A later image of Dysart shipyard with a smaller ship on the stocks with the harbour-master's house in the background and the small white hut for the pilots and stowers in the foreground. The harbour was still a busy place when this photograph was taken in the 1920s, with the shipyard's drawing loft and blacksmith's shop in the background.

The Abden shipyard at Kinghorn was established by John Key in 1863 just to the east of the parish church. In 1886 the yard built its first ship entirely from iron, the barque *River Tay*. The yard built a large number of vessels with orders from London, Glasgow, Leith and Dundee as well as overseas orders from Spain, Malta, Singapore and – perhaps surprisingly for such a small yard – twenty ships for Australia.

This image of Kinghorn taken from the Braes shows the shipyard on the right as well as several factory chimneys. One Kinghorn woman recalled that her father had worked at the Abden yard as a young man and travelled with the ship to its destination in Australia; once delivered, he was told that he would have to find his own way back to Scotland!

This aerial view of Burntisland shipyard, founded by William and Amos Ayre from Tyneside in 1918, was taken before the Second World War. The shipyard went into liquidation in 1968, primarily over contract difficulties on the *Ohrmazd* which led to punitive financial penalties which the yard simply could not overcome. Two more ships, *Christiane Bolton* and *Helen Miller* were built in 1969 before the yard closed down.

MV *Maltese Prince* was built by Burntisland Shipbuilding Company Ltd in 1946, one of a series of ships built at the yard for the Prince Line including *Scottish Prince, Cyprian Prince, Northumbrian Prince* and *Egyptian Prince*. The shipyard built 310 ships during its fifty years' lifetime.

The paddle steamer *Stirling Castle* was built in 1899 at Kinghorn shipyard, which by then had been taken over by J. Scott & Company. A slightly smaller version of her sister ship *Tantallon Castle*, her last voyage was to the Mediterranean when she was sunk near Malta after an explosion in September 1916.

Andrew Dryburgh served his apprenticeship as a shipbuilder before signing on as crew on the maiden voyage to China of the *Cutty Sark* in 1870, when she brought the fashionable new tea crop back to Britain. He was harbourmaster at Dysart for many years and took over the shipyard in 1904.

The harbourmaster's house was more recently used as the clubhouse for Dysart Sailing Club before it fell into disrepair. It was carefully restored in 2006 and is now the headquarters of Fife Cultural Trust.

Andrew Dryburgh brought a small doll back from China for his granddaughter, Mrs Curran, a gift she cherished for many years. The *Cutty Sark* was built on the Clyde in 1869 and took part in one of the most famous tea races of the period against the *Thermopylae*.

5

TEXTILES

Bridge Street, Dunfermline

Dunfermline was famous for its fine quality table and bed linen. Erskine Beveridge bought St Leonard's factory in the late 1880s and later expanded his factories to Cowdenbeath, Ladybank and Dunshalt. There were three silk mills in Dunfermline at one time including Winterthur Silks located in the former J&T Alexander linen mill at Canmore Works. The company made the silk for the then Princess Elizabeth's wedding dress in 1947.

The West Spinning Mill in Kirkcaldy was built as a flax spinning mill in 1806 by Messrs F. and W. Hendry, with the nearby Tiel Burn supplying the power for the machines. It was later taken over by Forth and Clyde Roperie and was sensitively restored as the Foyer in 1995 by the Link Housing Association.

Kirkcaldy Civic Society have erected a plaque at the entrance of the Foyer to mark its origins as a busy working mill. The building has many striking architectural features including a mansard roof, cast-iron Doric colonnade, arched doorway and decorative niches which were able to be maintained during the renovation.

Philp's mill at the west end of Kirkcaldy was powered entirely by water from the nearby Tiel Burn and not (as with later factories in the area) by steam. The spindle from the big waterwheel from Philp's factory was saved when the old factory was demolished and is now set in the wall as a reminder of the industry.

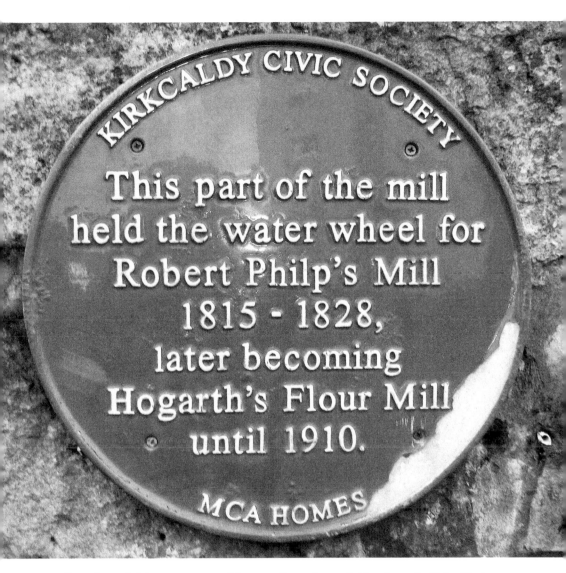

KIRKCALDY CIVIC SOCIETY

This part of the mill held the water wheel for Robert Philp's Mill 1815 - 1828, later becoming Hogarth's Flour Mill until 1910.

MCA HOMES

Baillie Robert Philp's water-powered linen mill stood near Bridge Street in Kirkcaldy in the nineteenth century. He collected linen from home weavers all over Fife and took it to the markets, and in 1815 bought the mill along with its bleach fields and dye works. A commemorative plaque was placed on the site which is now occupied by a new housing development.

Robert Philp provided education for the poorest children in the area by building three schools in Kirkcaldy and one in Kinghorn, and providing free clothing and books. His gravestone in Kirkcaldy's Old Kirk must be unique as the inscription includes the amount of his earthly assets, which amounted to £70,000.

This building was originally Philp's school in Kirkcaldy and is currently a nightclub. The Linktown school (now demolished) was surmounted by a statue of Philp with a child on each side. Philp knew the benefit of education for youngsters and through his philanthropy, children started school at 6 and most stayed until they were 15 and ready to go out to work.

Linen workers in Dysart are pictured here on their annual outing, when workers and their families paraded to the local railway station with flags and streamers led by a brass band. It was a day for people to dress in their best clothes as they walked from the factory gates to the station en route for Perth or Edinburgh.

The Pleasence. Falkland.

The Royal Burgh of Falkland had a long history of weaving, starting from the days of handloom weaving when the work was done at home in domestic cottages. The SCWS Pleasence linen factory, said to have been the most up-to-date weaving shed in the area, closed in 1960 with the loss of seventy jobs.

Local handloom weaver John Paterson carved the Man in the Rock sculpture in Dysart from natural soft sandstone, inspired by Byron's *Prisoner of Chillon*. His patient work was carried out on his way to and from work until he finished it in 1851. Over the years the statue was gradually eroded and finally crumbled away in 1970.

Wemyss School of Needlework was founded in the 1870s in Coaltown of Wemyss by Lady Henry Grosvenor. She established a sewing school in Wemyss Castle, later moving it to the present building, where village girls were trained in needlework, embroidery and smocking. 'We learned how to do crewel work, white work, wool tapestry and embroidery,' recalled one early worker. 'It was difficult at first until you got used to it but we had an excellent training.'

This little dress with its beautiful and painstaking stitching is a sample of the work done by the workers for aristocratic families. The girls were strictly disciplined and had to look after their hands to keep them smooth so that they could produce beautiful skilled work. 'You put your name down and I was accepted when I was 14 and stayed for seven years,' recalled a former stitcher.

THE WEMYSS CASTLE
NEEDLEWORK SCHOOL
COALTOWN OF WEMYSS.

Manageress—MISS JANET RUSSELL.

ALL MANNER OF

Embroideries. Tapestry & Crewel Work.

MARKING OF EVERY DESCRIPTION, AND

WHITE SEAM TO THE MOST ELABORATE.

All Designing done in the School.

A contemporary advertisement for the School of Needlework with manageress Miss Janet Russell. The girls were taken on as apprentices and felt it was an honour to be trained there and to produce work for the gentry. 'You only used the treadle machine on long side seams on nightdresses,' said one former worker. 'Then you had to hem it all by hand; the ladies we worked for didn't want machine sewing.'

This amazingly detailed old photograph of Normand's weaving shed in Dysart High Street shows the huge machinery and overhead spindles needed to make linen and other cloth. When the factory was working at full strength the noise must have been deafening.

Girls in the weaving department of one of the linen factories take a welcome break from work to pose for the camera. They would have started at the factory straight from school, often as young as 14 years old, and their wages would contribute to the household economy.

Mill workers from one of the Dysart linen factories are pictured on their lunch break. These women were all much older than the girls in the previous image and had probably worked there all their adult lives, which for the woman in the centre of the back row must have been a considerable time.

This young woman stopped work for a few moments to face the camera. Like her colleagues, she would have started in the textile factory straight from school and would have been trained on the job until she was familiar with the complicated machinery in front of her.

Dysart was once home to several linen factories. The largest building was Normand's spinning mill with the works of J&A Terrace to the left. Dovecot Crescent houses on the shore were built by James Normand to house his workers, but were demolished in 1966 when the Coal Board needed more land for the colliery waste.

The Wemyss linen factory put up flags, streamers and bunting to celebrate royal occasions such as coronations or weddings. No factory these days would consider decorating a workplace but this was at an earlier time before health and safety issues were paramount.

Ann Ness from Kirkcaldy took time off from her work in one of the local mills to pose for a photograph. The image shows clearly the massive, noisy and complicated machines on which the girls produced such delicate material.

6

POTTERY

The distinctive kilns of David Methven & Sons' Kirkcaldy Pottery were a landmark in the Links area for many years until they were demolished after the factory closed down. The atmosphere when the coal-fired potteries were working at full blast must have been full of pollution.

Kirkcaldy had four main potteries including David Methven & Sons' Kirkcaldy Pottery in the Links area. Although most of the sprawling pottery buildings are long gone, part of the original curved wall still remains, with what would have been openings for the clay deliveries still visible.

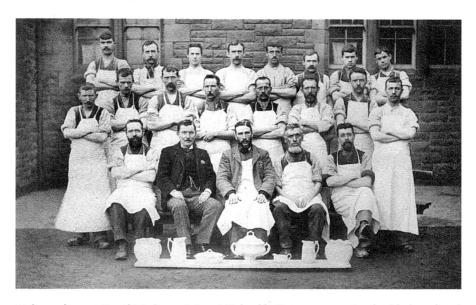

Male workers at David Methven & Sons' Kirkcaldy Pottery – wearing freshly laundered white aprons – are pictured with the pottery's last owner William Young in the front row and Andrew Forrester (later works manager) second from right in the centre row. A selection of their tureens, jugs and vases can be seen in the foreground.

Wemyss Ware cats, an example of which is painted here in tabby stripes, are extremely collectable today. As well as plain glazes such as yellow, green and pink, other favourite decorations were traditional pink roses, shamrocks, heart motifs and ribbon bows.

This beautiful Wemyss Ware ewer and basin set was decorated with purple and green irises and was made in Robert Heron's Fife Pottery in the Gallatown area of Kirkcaldy. The high prices which Wemyss pieces fetch at auction often soar to record levels.

Pottery pieces which were not up to the required standard either in the firing or decoration were put in the outside dumps where they were picked up and sold round the houses. Sisters Margaret and Isa McLeod are pictured with a clothes basket full of 'seconds' which they would sell for pocket money.

This amusing Wemyss white ceramic pig with pink ears and snout and complete with monocle and black top hat was probably originally made as an advertisement to go in a butcher's shop window. Large and small pigs were also made as decorative items or money boxes, and a pair of sleeping piglets sold in 2004 for £70,000.

This delicate Japan vase was painted with prunus blossom and swallows by Wemyss Ware master decorator Karel Nekola, whose two artist sons Joseph and Carl also worked in Fife Pottery. James Sharp, David Grinton and Edwin Sandland were other skilled decorators at the pottery who produced beautiful work.

Girls working in Methven's sponge-painting department around 1922. Seated from left to right are Adie Yule, Effie Waddell, Jenny Gourlay, Jenny Henderson and Kate Miller. They took small pieces of sponge which were cut into simple shapes and dipped them in paint before applying the designs to the plates.

This aerial view of Fife Pottery in Kirkcaldy shows the kilns and workshops where the now collectable Wemyss Ware was made. Pottery House, where owner Robert Heron lived, can be seen in the extreme top right corner of the photograph.

A group of mainly women workers in David Methven & Sons' Kirkcaldy Pottery in Links Street, with works manager Andrew Forrester in the centre. The girls obviously knew that the photographer was coming to the works, as many had put on smart dresses and all had taken great trouble with their hairstyles.

Although the pottery in the Links is long gone, this street sign still reminds us of the industry. The road was originally called Pottery Road, but as there was a Pottery Street in the Gallatown area of the town where Fife Pottery stood, it was altered to save confusion.

This little tunnel off Pratt Street is still there today and was originally used to transport clay from the clay field directly to Methven's pottery on a small rail or tram track – a simple and efficient way of getting the important raw material delivered to the door. Today school pupils from the nearby Balwearie High School use the tunnel as a useful shortcut to the High Street.

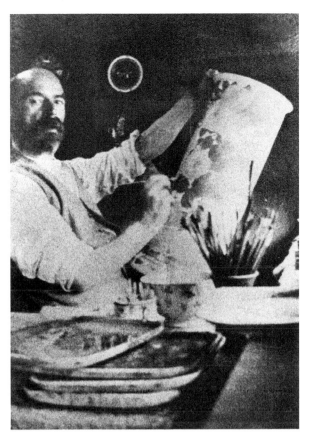

This old photograph shows the master Wemyss Ware decorator Karel Nekola painting a beautiful umbrella stand. Originally headhunted from Bohemia by Robert Heron, he settled in Kirkcaldy where he married and raised a family. His sons Carl and Joe followed in his footsteps as artists in Fife Pottery.

Nekola became disabled in his later years and was unable to go to the pottery. Despite this he was determined to keep painting and he utilised his garden shed as a workshop. Special pieces of ware were brought to him to be decorated and fired in a small kiln on his premises.

This fish tureen in the shape of a carp is one of the most highly prized pieces of Wemyss Ware because of its rarity. Its delicately curved shape, although very attractive, meant it rarely survived being taken out of the mould without breakage. The tureen had a little lid with a miniature fish on the top.

Workers at Methven's pottery had a summer excursion by charabanc where they had a trip into the country and a meal out, courtesy of their employers. The group included Ann Dewar, a skilled pottery gilder in the works, whose husband Henry was a sign writer with the charabanc firm General Motor Carrying Company.

7

GOLF

Edward, Prince of Wales (later King Edward VIII) is pictured here playing on the Old Course during his visit to St Andrews in 1934, with Forgan's golf shop on the far right. He received the Freedom of St Andrews in 1922 when he was appointed Captain of the Royal and Ancient Golf Club.

Above: Legendary St Andrews golfer 'Old' Tom Morris is pictured here on the Old Course in St Andrews beside the Swilcan Bridge. Born in St Andrews in 1821, he won four Open Championships between 1861 and 1867, and played in every British Open until 1895. His vast experience of the game allowed him to design golf courses in different parts of the country.

Opposite above: 'Old' Tom Morris is pictured outside his golf shop beside the Old Course overlooking the 18th green at St Andrews. He manufactured his own golf clubs and balls and reconditioned old golf balls. His son 'Young' Tom was also a gifted player who won four Opens in succession.

Opposite below: Golf club manufacturers A&G Spalding opened their Monro Works in Dysart in 1915 in the premises of a former linen works. It hasn't been determined how long this factory remained open in Dysart, but this was the first factory to be opened in the UK by the company which became internationally known for its sports equipment.

Two golfing legends played an exhibition match at Balwearie Golf Club in Kirkcaldy in June 1914. Henry Vardon (front, third from left), who had won the Open Championship for the sixth time, played George Duncan (front, second from right), who won the Open six years later. Balwearie was described in a contemporary guidebook as being laid out 'with a fine quality of turf from the neighbouring estate of Kirlrie; and with membership open to ladies, to whom special privileges have been extended as an encouragement to join.'

The Royal and Ancient Golf Club in St Andrews was founded in May 1754 and has since become the goal for golfers from around the world. The clubhouse, whose foundation stone was laid in 1853, is an iconic building recognised worldwide. St Andrews Links Trust is a charity which is responsible for the management of the Links courses, including the legendary Old Course.

R. & A. GOLF CLUB HOUSE & 18TH GREEN, ST. ANDREWS.   A.778

Another view of the Royal and Ancient Clubhouse. Taken around the 1930s, it shows the 18th green of the Old Course which has seen countless dramatic moments, particularly in the Open Championships including the 144th, which was played there in 2015. The Martyrs Monument and what was then the Grand Hotel are also pictured.

Elie Golf House Club is home to Elie and Earslferry Ladies Golf Club and Earlsferry Thistle Golf Club. Established in 1875, it still retains its sense of history, right down to the wooden lockers which once housed the golfing jackets of the nineteenth century. Legendary golfer James Braid, five times Open Champion between 1901 and 1910, learned to play on this course.

Opposite above: Players on the 14th green at the Old Course, St Andrews, watched by a crowd of spectators. The railway footbridge has long gone, as indeed has the line to St Andrews. As early as 1691, St Andrews was described as 'the metropolis of golf' and since then has been regarded as golf's spiritual home.

Opposite below: Dysart Golf Club, near Kirkcaldy, was inaugurated in 1898 as a 9-hole course situated to the left of Dysart cemetery. The first ball was played off by J. Oswald of Dunnikier House. The clubhouse was extended to a two-storey building before the course was taken over in 1950 and houses built on the site.

The 'Himalayas' putting green adjacent to the Old Course, owned by St Andrews Ladies Putting Club, was founded as a private club in 1867 but is now open to the public. Its popularity demonstrates that everyone can enjoy the pleasure of golf at St Andrews, no matter how inexperienced.

8

LINOLEUM

This aerial view illustrates the number of factories there were in the east of Kirkcaldy in the early twentieth century, with a wide spread of buildings and their tall chimneys and Nairn's factory visible on the beach at Pathhead Sands. When Michael Nairn built his factory in 1847, it was known locally as 'Nairn's Folly' as it was seen at the time as a loss-maker since it manufactured what was considered to be new-fangled floorcloth. His plan included south-facing windows so that the floorcloth could be dried in the sun.

Nairn's St Mary's canvas factory on the Path in Kirkcaldy had 1,870 looms worked by steam power. Once a huge source of employment in the town, it is now derelict but the façade of the listed building remains, including the stone plaque which reads M Nairn & Co. on the front. It was situated conveniently near the harbour where there was a steady trade in imports of cork and linseed oil and exports of linoleum.

The original tower of Nairn's St Mary's canvas factory, left, far background, still remains on the Path. The tower's height was essential to linoleum production as the huge lengths of linoleum were hung from the ceiling to dry off. Michael Nairn built his first canvas factory in 1828 in Coal Wynd at the top of his garden.

This image shows one of Michael Nairn's linoleum works in Victoria Road when work on the Victoria viaduct in 1899 was taking place. It lay empty for many years and despite a campaign to keep the listed building intact and find other uses for it, the factory building was demolished in 2014.

The classical red sandstone frontage of Nairn's offices on the Path in Kirkcaldy can be seen on the left, with factories on both sides of the street. Work was being carried out in 1965 to widen and improve the Path which was a steep gradient and a hazard to earlier horse transport even though it had been straightened and improved on several occasions including in 1902, when it became a tramcar route.

The buildings of Barry, Ostlere and Shepherd Ltd, another Kirkcaldy floorcloth producer, can be seen here behind Kirkcaldy Museum and War Memorial Gardens before the library building was added. The works were deliberately sited next to the main railway line for ease of transport. The firm was an amalgamation of two earlier companies, Kirkcaldy Linoleum Company Ltd and John Barry, Ostlere and Company Ltd. There were several groups to cater for workers' leisure time including football, golf and horticulture.

The sprawling buildings which made up the offices of Barry, Ostlere and Shepherd Ltd were once thriving places, but were unused after the firm closed down. Their range of linoleum was advertised as ideal for shipping, hospitals, trains, hotels and domestic premises. For a short time the premises housed an interesting industrial museum but when that closed the premises were used as Fife Council offices and, at the time of writing, are empty and awaiting redevelopment.

Workers at Barry, Ostlere and Shepherd Ltd took part in the annual Hospital Pageant in Kirkcaldy in 1924 to raise funds before the advent of the National Health Service. Not only was their lorry decorated to promote the firm's products but the girls' dresses were also made out of linoleum. Many other firms and individuals took part in the pageant, which was a popular event in the town.

The quiet village of Falkland seems an unlikely place for a linoleum factory, but Scottish Co-operative Wholesale Society manufactured lino here from 1919 until 1963, when Smith Anderson took over the site to make paper bags and other related products.

Overleaf: This 1923 image shows workers in the lithographic machine room of the Allen Lithographic Company Ltd printing pattern books for the linoleum industry, not only for local factories but for most of the lino manufacturers throughout the UK. The large printing plant which stretched from Townsend Place to Church Street has since been turned into housing.

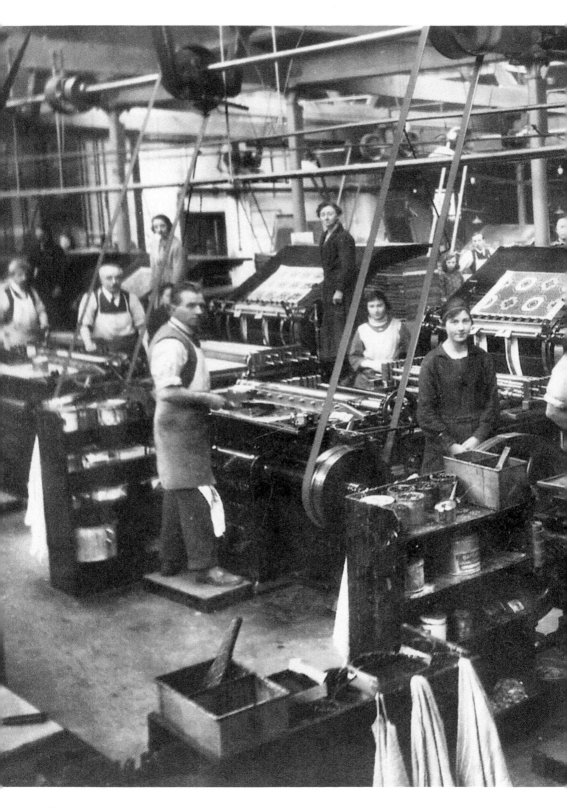

One of linen manufacturer Robert Philp's schools was in Nether Street. When the school closed in 1892, Nairn's expanded their linoleum works and built right round it; when the factory was demolished in 1967, the school building with its commemorative plaque was still intact.

9

TOURISM

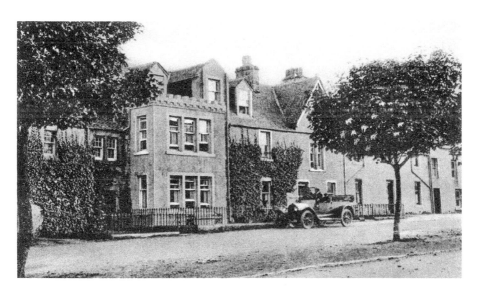

The historic and former Royal Burgh of Crail has always been popular with tourists. The Forelands in the town's Marketgate was built in 1759 as a private house. By the early 1930s it had become a hotel, advertising as 'Board Residence, excellent cuisine, home comforts and first class service.'

High Street, Leven

St Andrews, a favourite holiday destination then as now, is pictured with bathing huts drawn up on the sandy beach so that Edwardian visitors could change from their outdoor clothes into bathing costumes and still retain their modesty.

Opposite above: The Golf Hotel on Crail's High Street gave quick access to the beach and picturesque harbour. The town has retained many of its historic buildings including the Tolbooth, which was originally built in the sixteenth century and altered over the course of the years. Crail was made a Royal Burgh in 1310 by Robert the Bruce who also gave it the right to hold markets on Sundays.

Opposite below: The Caledonian Hotel on Leven High Street advertised 'Stabling and Garage' on its gable end, with a regular railway service to St Andrews and the popular tramway service passing its door. When Kirkcaldy trams stopped running in 1931, Wemyss and District Tramway bought some of their double-decker rolling stock to add to their own fleet of yellow single-deck trams.

A typical summer's day on St Andrews beach around the 1930s, with what was then the Grand Hotel in the background beside the Royal and Ancient Golf Club. Youngsters – and one enthusiastic mother on the right – were happily digging holes in the sand: perhaps the weather was warmer in those days?

Burntisland beach was crowded with holidaymakers in the 1930s and '40s, with small boats giving pleasure trips round the bay. The proximity of the railway line gave easy access for visitors, and travellers on steam trains would get an excellent view of the beach.

Kirkcaldy station, seen here with a steam train approaching, was a convenient starting point for local people who went on holiday to the East Fife resorts. It was then part of a direct line to St Andrews but this was discontinued along with many other routes under the Beeching cuts in the early 1960s.

A group of locals pictured at the west end of Leuchars beside the railway level crossing and the passenger bridge. The hotel was ideally placed for tourists making their holiday journey by train. The Leven to Thornton Junction railway route was closed to freight in 1966 and to passenger traffic three years later.

Shortage of money did not mean that holidays were out of the question, and the Fife coast was a popular spot for alfresco camping. The local paper in 1911 reported: 'There are over 200 young men from Glasgow, Airdrie and Edinburgh in tents on the shore, a record number. They have called their camps the Jolly Boys, the Woodbines, or the Naughty Boys.'

Opposite above: A peaceful street scene showing the houses with their typical outside stairs in Aberdour, a favourite holiday spot with its sandy beach and convenient rail links. For many years it was two distinctly separate villages, Easter and Wester Aberdour, one on each side of the Dour Burn.

Opposite below: Kinghorn beach was always crowded with locals and visitors on sunny days, despite its proximity to the local shipyard and factories. It was a favourite spot for touring companies of pierrots who drew appreciative audiences.

High Street, Aberdour

THE SANDS FROM THE BRAES, KINGHORN.

Edwardian ladies take a leisurely stroll along St Andrews pier, with St Rule's Tower and the cathedral in the background. The tall Royal George tenement has the gasworks chimney behind it, and the neighbouring Bell Rock Tavern was run by the Bissett family in the late 1890s. The harbour walk has been a traditional event for students at St Andrews University for many years.

10

SHOPS

Buckhaven Co-operative Society's large store in Randolph Street was established in 1869 and had no fewer than seventeen departments which catered for every need including bakery, grocery, drapers, tailoring, millinery, boot repairing, paperhanging as well as funeral undertaking.

Kirkcaldy High Street around the 1960s when the traffic was still two-way, with Burton's art-deco style store on the corner and a mixture of shops including Bata Shoes, Grieve's, Brighter Homes and Hardy's furniture shop.

Opposite above: Mrs Hamilton's china shop at 223 Links Street in Kirkcaldy, with a small window display of decorative cups, saucers, plates and vases. No doubt she would have stocked a wide selection of pottery items made in David Methven & Sons' Kirkcaldy Pottery just along the road.

Opposite below: An early image of the Port Brae, Kirkcaldy, showing Gillies' large furniture shop on the right and the Victoria Bar on the left. There was a mixture of transport available then; the tramlines were still there and early cars were beginning to take over from the traditional horse and cart. St James's church in the background was demolished to make way for road widening.

A busy shopping day on Dunfermline's High Street around the 1940s with the nineteenth-century Town House in the background. Shops included Hepworths men's tailors on the corner, Woolworth's which had originally been on the other side of the street, and the Bank of Scotland.

Opposite above: The Co-operative Society's store at Coaltown of Wemyss was typical of the widespread network of the society's shops in towns and villages. The Co-operative movement started in the nineteenth century, buying from local farmers, who were given a guaranteed market, and selling at affordable prices to its members. Its regular dividends were lifelines to many people at the time.

Opposite below: Mrs Mavor's Millinery Warehouse in Dysart sold not only hats but a wide variety of clothes and underwear – including the serviceable heavy 'drawers' displayed on the shop doorway – for both children and adults.

Store. Coaltown of Wemyss.

James Page's shop in Cupar proclaimed he was a family grocer and wine merchant, and his advertising displays included high class tea, 'Grand old Scotch Whisky' (at 1s 8d a bottle) and naphtha soap, with the motto on the front of the shop proclaiming 'If you want anything special, try Page'. Deliveries were made to customers by horse and cart.

Opposite: The bakery department of Dysart Co-operative Society was one of several bakers in the former Royal Burgh. As well as the advertisement in the window for wedding and christening cakes, there is also a poster calling for 'A Living Wage – Unity is Strength'.

Above: The seaside town of Lundin Links had a comprehensive general store on the corner of Leven Road, with adverts for chocolate and cocoa in the window as well as incorporating a post office and a drycleaning agency.

Opposite above: An early advertisement for Robert Milliken, portrait and landscape photographer. The Kirkcaldy firm, established in 1864, offered a range of services including outdoor and architectural work, lantern slides and even copies of paintings.

Right: I.J. McEwen's little shop selling chocolate, confectionary and cigarettes was typical of the small shops which were situated in one room of the proprietor's house. A wooden table would be pressed into use as a counter, and the shopkeeper only had to take a few steps to the kitchen for her dinner.

Above: The Ice Cream Warehouse at 299 High Street in Kirkcaldy's Port Brae is pictured here around 1900, when many Italian families came to Scotland to introduce their delicious ice cream. The shop is listed in the 1906 Trade Directory as owned by Guiseppe Soave and by 1936 it had passed on to the next generation of the family and was run by Miss Catherine Soave.

Opposite above: Edward Descamps from Belgium posed outside his Kirkcaldy garage and showroom with one of his early touring cars. He also had premises at the Olympia Arcade where he advertised as 'Agents for Mercedes' and, for those with less expensive tastes, 'Bicycles for Hire'.

Opposite below: William Johnston is listed in a 1924 Trade Directory as having a carriage-hiring business at 117 Market Street, St Andrews, charging 4s 6d for hiring a lorry for the day. He also had premises at 104 North Street, which were demolished in 1974.

David H. Fowler's shop at 69 High Street, Dysart, was basically a newsagent and tobacconist, but as well as advertisements for daily papers and pipe tobacco, the window display had an eclectic mix of stock including rubber stamps, buckets, picture postcards and babies' rattles.

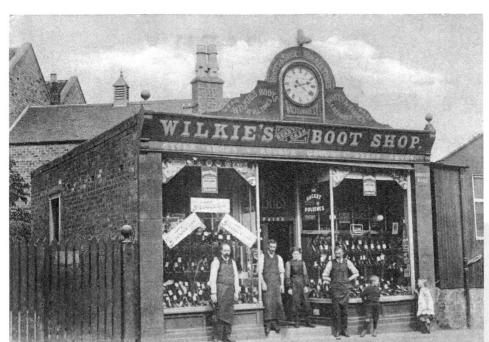

Opposite: Wilkie's Boot Shop had a branch in Mid Street, Kirkcaldy, as well as this building at 66 Dunnikier Road. They advertised that their boots and shoes – which included cycle shoes and dress shoes – were correct for quality, comfort and wear.

Below: Kirk Wynd in Kirkcaldy with the old kirk at the top of the hill had shops including Payne's Boot Depot on the right with a notice saying 'Terms Cash. Repairs Neatly Done'. One of the youngsters is delivering a basket with bottles of beer.

The west end of Kirkcaldy at the junction of Nicol Street and High Street, with a horse and delivery cart outside the distinctive curved building of the Links Bread Society and the imposing Wemyss Buildings. Youngsters (including one small boy in a miniature sailor suit and hat) and passers-by posed for this photographer in the 1900s.

If you enjoyed this book, you may also be interested in…

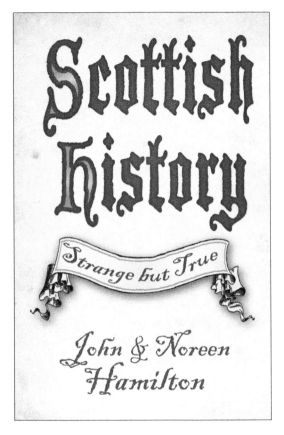

Scottish History
Strange but True

JOHN & NOREEN HAMILTON

978 0 7509 6630 6

This book contains hundreds of 'strange but true' stories about Scottish history. Arranged into a miniature history of Scotland, and with bizarre and hilarious true tales for every era, it will delight anyone with an interest in Scotland's past.

Visit our website and discover thousands of other History Press books.

www.thehistorypress.co.uk

If you enjoyed this book, you may also be interested in…

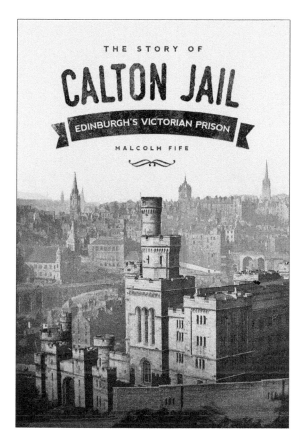

The Story of Calton Jail
Edinburgh's Victorian Prison

MALCOLM FIFE

978 0 7509 6224 7

Located a short distance from Edinburgh's Princes Street, the castellated design of Calton Prison was often mistaken by nineteenth-century visitors to the city for Edinburgh Castle. Occupying a prominent site on the rocky slope of Calton Hill, the then largest jail in Scotland was constructed to replace the ageing tolbooth and soon became the region's main correction facility, housing prisoners awaiting trial and those facing execution, including murderers, political agitators, fraudsters, terrorists and even the notorious bodysnatchers Burke and Hare. In this, the first long-overdue history of the prison, Malcolm Fife tells the story of Calton Jail, the staff and prisoners, the escapes and executions, and the crimes and punishments. Richly illustrated, it offers an absorbing insight into the Scottish criminal justice system of yesteryear.

Visit our website and discover thousands of other History Press books.

www.thehistorypress.co.uk

If you enjoyed this book, you may also be interested in...

The Scotland Colouring Book

978 0 7509 6781 5

If you love Scotland, then you will love colouring it in! Scotland has charmed visitors for centuries, and this collection of intricate illustrations is a celebration of its unique appeal. Featuring a range of picturesque vistas, from freshwater lochs and wooded glens to majestic mountains, granite cities and medieval castles, each stunning scene is full of intriguing detail sure to fire the imagination and make you reach for your colouring pencils. There are absolutely no rules – you can choose any combination of colours you like to bring these wonderful images to life.

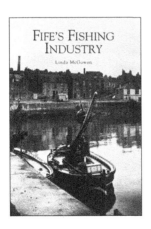

Fife's Fishing Industry

LINDA MCGOWAN

978 0 7524 2795 9

This book charts the evolution of Fife's fishing industry through photographs held at the Scottish Fisheries Museum in Anstruther. They cover the period from the 1880s to the present day and inevitably concentrate on the East Neuk fishing villages that dominated Fife's fishing industry. In these images we can see the harbours teeming with boats, the piers busy with herring lasses gutting and packing the fish, carters and coopers, and the shores piled high with baskets and boxes, all revolving around the silver harvest of the sea.

Visit our website and discover thousands of other History Press books.

www.thehistorypress.co.uk